MW01600828

FIRST DAY & LAST DAY

SCHOOL MEMORY ALBUM
K-12

This Book Belongs To:

_____

BOOKS

FIRST DAY OF GRADE ___

STUDENT WAS FEELING

_____

_____

Insert Photo

PARENTS WERE FEELING

_____

_____

TODAY'S WEATHER IS

_____

WHAT WE HAD FOR BREAKFAST

_____

THIS YEAR'S TEACHER(S) WILL BE

_____

Have a Great Year!

LAST DAY OF GRADE ____

STUDENT WAS FEELING

_____

_____

PARENTS WERE FEELING

_____

_____

TODAY'S WEATHER IS

_____

WHAT WE HAD FOR BREAKFAST

_____

THE BEST MEMORY FROM THIS YEAR

_____

Have a Great Summer!

Insert Photo

FIRST DAY OF GRADE ___

STUDENT WAS FEELING

_____

_____

PARENTS WERE FEELING

_____

_____

TODAY'S WEATHER IS

_____

WHAT WE HAD FOR BREAKFAST

_____

THIS YEAR'S TEACHER(S) WILL BE

_____

Have a Great Year!

Insert Photo

LAST DAY OF GRADE ____

STUDENT WAS FEELING

_____

_____

Insert Photo

PARENTS WERE FEELING

_____

_____

TODAY'S WEATHER IS

_____

WHAT WE HAD FOR BREAKFAST

_____

THE BEST MEMORY FROM THIS YEAR

_____

Have a Great Summer!

FIRST DAY OF GRADE ___

STUDENT WAS FEELING

_____

_____

Insert Photo

PARENTS WERE FEELING

_____

_____

TODAY'S WEATHER IS

_____

WHAT WE HAD FOR BREAKFAST

_____

THIS YEAR'S TEACHER(S) WILL BE

_____

Have a Great Year!

LAST DAY OF GRADE ____

STUDENT WAS FEELING

_____

_____

PARENTS WERE FEELING

_____

_____

TODAY'S WEATHER IS

_____

WHAT WE HAD FOR BREAKFAST

_____

THE BEST MEMORY FROM THIS YEAR

_____

Have a Great Summer!

Insert Photo

FIRST DAY OF GRADE ___

STUDENT WAS FEELING

_____

_____

PARENTS WERE FEELING

_____

_____

TODAY'S WEATHER IS

_____

WHAT WE HAD FOR BREAKFAST

_____

THIS YEAR'S TEACHER(S) WILL BE

_____

Have a Great Year!

Insert Photo

LAST DAY OF GRADE ___

STUDENT WAS FEELING

_____

_____

PARENTS WERE FEELING

_____

_____

TODAY'S WEATHER IS

_____

WHAT WE HAD FOR BREAKFAST

_____

THE BEST MEMORY FROM THIS YEAR

_____

Insert Photo

Have a Great Summer!

FIRST DAY OF GRADE ___

STUDENT WAS FEELING

_____

_____

Insert Photo

PARENTS WERE FEELING

_____

_____

TODAY'S WEATHER IS

_____

WHAT WE HAD FOR BREAKFAST

_____

THIS YEAR'S TEACHER(S) WILL BE

_____

Have a Great Year!

LAST DAY OF GRADE ___

STUDENT WAS FEELING

_____

_____

Insert Photo

PARENTS WERE FEELING

_____

_____

TODAY'S WEATHER IS

_____

WHAT WE HAD FOR BREAKFAST

_____

THE BEST MEMORY FROM THIS YEAR

_____

Have a Great Summer!

FIRST DAY OF GRADE ___

STUDENT WAS FEELING

_____

_____

PARENTS WERE FEELING

_____

_____

TODAY'S WEATHER IS

_____

WHAT WE HAD FOR BREAKFAST

_____

THIS YEAR'S TEACHER(S) WILL BE

_____

Have a Great Year!

Insert Photo

LAST DAY OF GRADE ___

STUDENT WAS FEELING

_____

_____

PARENTS WERE FEELING

_____

_____

TODAY'S WEATHER IS

_____

WHAT WE HAD FOR BREAKFAST

_____

THE BEST MEMORY FROM THIS YEAR

_____

Have a Great Summer!

Insert Photo

FIRST DAY OF GRADE ___

STUDENT WAS FEELING

_____

_____

Insert Photo

PARENTS WERE FEELING

_____

_____

TODAY'S WEATHER IS

_____

WHAT WE HAD FOR BREAKFAST

_____

THIS YEAR'S TEACHER(S) WILL BE

_____

Have a Great Year!

LAST DAY OF GRADE ____

STUDENT WAS FEELING

_____

_____

PARENTS WERE FEELING

_____

_____

TODAY'S WEATHER IS

_____

WHAT WE HAD FOR BREAKFAST

_____

THE BEST MEMORY FROM THIS YEAR

_____

Have a Great Summer!

Insert Photo

FIRST DAY OF GRADE ___

STUDENT WAS FEELING

_____

_____

Insert Photo

PARENTS WERE FEELING

_____

_____

TODAY'S WEATHER IS

_____

WHAT WE HAD FOR BREAKFAST

_____

THIS YEAR'S TEACHER(S) WILL BE

_____

Have a Great Year!

LAST DAY OF GRADE ___

STUDENT WAS FEELING

_____

_____

PARENTS WERE FEELING

_____

_____

TODAY'S WEATHER IS

_____

WHAT WE HAD FOR BREAKFAST

_____

THE BEST MEMORY FROM THIS YEAR

_____

Have a Great Summer!

Insert Photo

First Day of Grade ___

Student Was Feeling

_____

_____

Parents Were Feeling

_____

_____

Today's Weather Is

_____

What We Had For Breakfast

_____

This Year's Teacher(s) Will Be

_____

Have a Great Year!

Insert Photo

LAST DAY OF GRADE ____

STUDENT WAS FEELING

_____

_____

PARENTS WERE FEELING

_____

_____

TODAY'S WEATHER IS

_____

WHAT WE HAD FOR BREAKFAST

_____

THE BEST MEMORY FROM THIS YEAR

_____

Insert Photo

Have a Great Summer!

FIRST DAY OF GRADE ___

STUDENT WAS FEELING

_____

_____

PARENTS WERE FEELING

_____

_____

TODAY'S WEATHER IS

_____

WHAT WE HAD FOR BREAKFAST

_____

THIS YEAR'S TEACHER(S) WILL BE

_____

Insert Photo

Have a Great Year!

LAST DAY OF GRADE ____

STUDENT WAS FEELING

_____

_____

PARENTS WERE FEELING

_____

_____

TODAY'S WEATHER IS

_____

WHAT WE HAD FOR BREAKFAST

_____

THE BEST MEMORY FROM THIS YEAR

_____

Have a Great Summer!

Insert Photo

FIRST DAY OF GRADE ___

STUDENT WAS FEELING

_____

_____

Insert Photo

PARENTS WERE FEELING

_____

_____

TODAY'S WEATHER IS

_____

WHAT WE HAD FOR BREAKFAST

_____

THIS YEAR'S TEACHER(S) WILL BE

_____

Have a Great Year!

LAST DAY OF GRADE ___

STUDENT WAS FEELING

_____

_____

PARENTS WERE FEELING

_____

_____

TODAY'S WEATHER IS

_____

WHAT WE HAD FOR BREAKFAST

_____

THE BEST MEMORY FROM THIS YEAR

_____

Have a Great Summer!

Insert Photo

FIRST DAY OF GRADE ___

STUDENT WAS FEELING

_____

_____

Insert Photo

PARENTS WERE FEELING

_____

_____

TODAY'S WEATHER IS

_____

WHAT WE HAD FOR BREAKFAST

_____

THIS YEAR'S TEACHER(S) WILL BE

_____

Have a Great Year!

LAST DAY OF GRADE ____

STUDENT WAS FEELING

_____

_____

Insert Photo

PARENTS WERE FEELING

_____

_____

TODAY'S WEATHER IS

_____

WHAT WE HAD FOR BREAKFAST

_____

THE BEST MEMORY FROM THIS YEAR

_____

Have a Great Summer!

FIRST DAY OF GRADE ___

STUDENT WAS FEELING

_____

_____

PARENTS WERE FEELING

_____

_____

TODAY'S WEATHER IS

_____

WHAT WE HAD FOR BREAKFAST

_____

THIS YEAR'S TEACHER(S) WILL BE

_____

Have a Great Year!

Insert Photo

LAST DAY OF GRADE ___

STUDENT WAS FEELING

_____

_____

PARENTS WERE FEELING

_____

_____

TODAY'S WEATHER IS

_____

WHAT WE HAD FOR BREAKFAST

_____

THE BEST MEMORY FROM THIS YEAR

_____

Have a Great Summer!

Insert Photo

NOTES AND PHOTOS

NOTES AND PHOTOS

NOTES AND PHOTOS

NOTES AND PHOTOS

Notes and Photos

NOTES AND PHOTOS

Made in the USA
Monee, IL
18 May 2025

17672521R00020